'BLESSED MILAN
PROUD AND PASSIONATE WOMAN
WITH TWO LOVING BREASTS
READY TO NOURISH THE PEOPLES
OF THE WORLD.'

PER MILANO, ALDA MERINI (1931-2009)

There are cities where I could live, and others I wouldn't even if I was paid to. There are cities I fall hopelessly in love with and then forget about in an instant, like the most ungrateful of lovers. And then, there's Milan.

Milan has a strong character: it either adopts you or rejects you, there's no compromise. It makes you feel at the centre of the world or completely out of step, embraces you and, the next moment, ignores you. It's fast, frenzied, always hungry, maternal. This isn't a city that reveals itself at first glance. You need to learn to observe it, listen to it, follow its rhythm. Those who find it grey have never lingered long enough to grasp all its nuances. Those who find it cold have simply never found the parts of it that resonate with them.

This book is neither a comprehensive guide nor a list of addresses to tick off like a checklist. It's the story of a city experienced daily, through its hidden gems, its authentic flavours, its places inviting you to stay a moment and those you'll barely brush against. You'll find my favourite spots, those I recommend to friends, those I always return to and those I'm still discovering.

Describing Milan in just 30 experiences was a challenge – and I cheated: the numbers don't exactly correspond to the places I'm going to tell you about, because in reality, there are so many

Soul of Milan

A GUIDE TO EXCEPTIONAL EXPERIENCES

WRITTEN BY MARGHERITA DEVALLE
PHOTOS BY OTTAVIO FANTIN

JONGLEZ PUBLISHING

Travel guides

more. Milan is a mosaic, a city that changes mood depending on what time it went to bed the night before.

Here, you can live by the rules or shake them up, pretend to be a grand lady or a vagabond, because Milan is both at once. At one crossroads, it'll make you think of Leonardo's *Lady with an Ermine*, and two streets down you'll feel like you're on the set of an apocalyptic film. It's a bit like drinking in the worst bar in Caracas after having dined on a Manhattan rooftop. And it's precisely this mix that makes this city so beautiful, just like those who inhabit it and who, instead of asking who you are, will want to know what you do. Milan will exhilarate you or annoy you, but it will never leave you indifferent.

Through these pages, I want to take you to the heart of this city, make you feel its frantic rhythm as well as its more intimate spots, between its unshakeable certainties and its hushed secrets shared only with those who pause to listen. Expect to find honest cuisine, surprising atmospheres, and places where you'll want to linger. For if Milan often gives the impression of not having a second to waste, this guide is an invitation to discover it without rushing. And perhaps, as you flip through the pages, you'll end up discovering its essence.

Margherita Devalle

This playlist tells the story of Milan through the songs of artists who have lived it, loved it, crossed it, or even just imagined it. I curated it like a soundtrack: to accompany the reading of these pages, but also your footsteps. To be listened to with eyes closed, while walking, riding a tram, hopping into a taxi, or in those moments when you pause to watch Milan unfold before your eyes like a film.

Urban explorer, author, radio host and podcaster, **Margherita Devalle**, aka Fatty Furba, leads international projects in music and travel. She lives and works in Milan, where she has made a name for herself thanks to her unique and innovative perspective. She can capture in just a few moments the essence of this Italian city where tradition and modernity constantly interact. All the while, she never ceases to explore and tell stories about the world.

A passionate street photographer, **Ottavio Fantin** has been capturing the energy of the city and the poetry of empty spaces since 2006, mainly using film photography. Based in Milan, he collaborates with major fashion brands and musical artists, both in Italy and internationally.

WHAT YOU WON'T FIND
IN THIS GUIDE

- All-you-can-eat buffet aperitifs
- The same old Duomo–Galleria–Montenapoleone tour and that's it
- Restaurants with menus translated in ten languages

WHAT YOU WILL FIND
IN THIS GUIDE

- The address of a typical old Milanese apartment where you can have dinner with strangers
- A rainbow hidden in a church
- A greengrocer who also makes cocktails
- Addresses of authentic Milanese trattorias
- A house filled with books that you can skim through for free
- The perfect sandwich to eat after midnight
- The pizzeria of a genius
- A reason to return, even if you think you've seen it all

KEY TO THE SYMBOLS USED IN
SOUL OF MILAN

Under
€20

Between
€20 and €50

More
than €50

Reservations
recommended

100%
Milanese

Opening times often vary,
so we recommend checking them directly
on the website of the place you plan to visit.

01. Dining in a private residence
02. A stunning contemporary art space
03. Riding in a legendary velodrome
04. A stylish bar with a vintage touch
05. The most breathtaking view of the city
06. A vinyl kiosk amidst the tourist traps
07. A wild night in Chinatown
08. A relaxing oasis of wellbeing
09. The magic of outdoor cinema
10. Pre-dinner drinks at a greengrocer's
11. A haircut by candle flame to strengthen the roots
12. Exceptional modern architecture housing Etruscan art
13. The best trattoria in town?
14. You'll want to explore again, even when it's time to leave
15. Over 35,000 books in a magical place
16. Milan By Night
17. A unique, intimate and extraordinary experience
18. Street food, Milan style
19. A secret temple in a restaurant basement
20. Visit one of the world's most beautiful libraries
21. Milan's best cocktail bars
22. Spend a day like a Milanese in the Navigli district
23. A brilliant pizzeria frozen in the 1970s
24. Listen to an improvised concert in a bookshop
25. Underground culture that is literally underground
26. A restaurant that has stood the test of time
27. Visit an exceptional museum without the crowds
28. Classic milanese cuisine
29. 20th-century art at your fingertips
30. A little-known Renaissance masterpiece

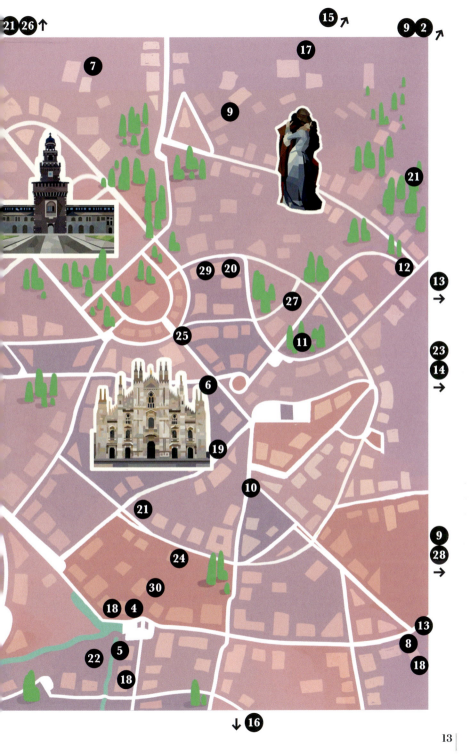

DINING IN
A PRIVATE RESIDENCE

Tucked away on the top floor of an old Milan apartment among the buildings of Via Padova, *Casa di Alfio* is a charming and intimate home restaurant. Welcoming yet refined, it features a table setting that changes with every meal.

Food, wine, sharing, music, and Nina – these are the five guiding principles of Alfio, born Alfredo Chirizzi. Here, you dine quite literally in his home.

Alfredo's journey began in fashion, where he spent years as a visual merchandiser for luxury brands. But everything changed with the birth of his daughter Nina, inspiring him to leave it all behind and dedicate himself to what truly makes him happy: cooking and sharing it with others. And so, *Alfio Sunday Service* was born.

To book this one-of-a-kind dining experience – shared with nine other guests, paired with natural wines and great music – you simply need to message him on Instagram. Each evening is unique, and what happens in this almost-secret venue often feels a little magical.

ALFIO SUNDAY SERVICE
SECRET ADDRESS

info@ciaoalfio.it

ciaoalfio.it
Instagram: @alfio_alfredochirizzi

€65 for a shared dinner,
price on request for a private dinner

A STUNNING CONTEMPORARY **ART SPACE**

For many, Pirelli HangarBicocca is simply one of the most breathtaking contemporary art venues – a must-visit in Milan. The extraordinary installation *The Seven Heavenly Palaces 2004-2015* by Anselm Kiefer would alone be worth the trip.

Housed in a former locomotive factory spanning 15,000 square metres, the space permanently showcases Kiefer's monumental work alongside a changing programme of exhibitions.

Be sure to spend a few minutes in the bookshop – small but impressively curated.

And if you need a break, the cosy bistro is perfect for lunch or an aperitivo.

PIRELLI HANGARBICOCCA
VIA CHIESE, 2
20126 MILANO

pirellihangarbicocca.org
Instagram: @pirelli_hangarbicocca

Free

RIDING IN A LEGENDARY VELODROME

1935. In the narrow streets of the Borg De Scigolatt, Milan's old market gardening district, a sporting icon was born: the Vigorelli Velodrome. Today, those with a cycling club licence – regardless from which country – have the rare privilege of being able to rent a track bike and ride on its historic wooden track, a listed monument.

The most curious explorers should seek out Niche 31, a hidden spot offering a glimpse of the velodrome's original structure.

Nicknamed *La Pista Magica* (The Magic Track), Vigorelli is also steeped in musical history, having hosted legendary concerts, including The Beatles' first-ever Italian gig in 1965 – commemorated by a golden plaque at the entrance – and Led Zeppelin in 1971. Not every concert went as planned, but that's another story …

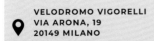

VELODROMO VIGORELLI
VIA ARONA, 19
20149 MILANO

vigorelli.eu
Instagram : @cvvigorelli

Visits: TUE and SAT, 5pm–7pm

Closed: August and bank holidays

A STYLISH BAR
WITH A VINTAGE TOUCH

Tucked away in a quiet corner of Porta Ticinese, The Doping Bar feels like a hidden gem from another era. With its leather trunks and vintage sports memorabilia, it exudes the atmosphere of an exclusive old-world club – somewhere between a classic American speakeasy and a quintessential British lounge.

Located inside the Aethos Milan hotel, this stylish bar is perfect for pre-dinner drinks or a late-night cocktail, with a drinks menu that's constantly evolving and an intimate, softly lit ambience.

For a touch of indulgence, don't miss the Sunday luxury brunch, featuring a DJ set and champagne – the ultimate way to round off the week.

THE DOPING BAR
PIAZZA VENTIQUATTRO MAGGIO, 8
20123 MILANO

dopingbar.it

Instagram: @the.doping

THE MOST BREATHTAKING VIEW
OF THE CITY

On the seventh floor of the 21 House of Stories Navigli hotel, open from spring to autumn, the rooftop bar I Mirador offers one of the most breathtaking views in all of Milan.

Here's how it works: book online (a must), then settle onto the cushions by the pool or head to the upper level – ideally just before sunset.

In front of you, the Darsena glows orange; to the left, San Siro Stadium; to the right, the shimmering Madonnina atop the Duomo.

Pure bliss.

I MIRADOR
VIA PRIVATA FRATELLI ANGELO E MARIO BETTINELLI, 3
20136 MILANO

Reservations:
imirador.superbexperience.com

Instagram: @imirador.milano

For groups of 8+ people:
booking@imirador.com

A VINYL KIOSK
AMIDST THE TOURIST TRAPS

On Piazza del Duomo, in the midst of tourist crowds and the mediocre shops catering to them, Gigi is a survivor. In 1977, he transformed the small kiosk he had inherited from his uncles into a sanctuary for vinyl enthusiasts.

Although after Expo 2015 he added a few souvenirs 'to keep up with the times', the heart of his kiosk remains intact: vintage vinyl records from all eras and genres, each catalogued by heart without any written archive. Every record is a unique piece. Among the kiosk's hidden treasures, try asking him for the sealed and never-opened Rino Gaetano vinyl, or ask him to tell you the story of selling a very rare Battiato. Among his customers are many VIPs; if you stay longer than the time it takes to drink a coffee, you might see some of them pass by ...

DISCOVERY BY GIGI
PASSAGGIO SANTA MARGHERITA
PIAZZA DEI MERCANTI
20123 MILANO

+39 339 699 9417

A WILD NIGHT IN CHINATOWN

Milan's Chinatown gives its New York counterpart a run for its money. But where should you go among the many options, some of which are best avoided?

> Start your visit with a glass of wine at **Cantine Isola**, a little slice of paradise tucked away in the neighbourhood's streets, where the walls are adorned with labels and bottles of excellent wines. If the weather allows, enjoy your drink outdoors, perched on typical red plastic stools in the purest Asian style. On Tuesdays, there are songs and poetry readings in the Milanese dialect.

> Across the street is the famous **Ravioleria Sarpi**, a must-visit spot: freshly prepared stuffed dumplings made right in front of you with quality ingredients and a touch of love. It is said that the best Chinese ravioli in the city are served here … You can even try to recreate them at home by signing up for one of their cooking classes.

CANTINE ISOLA
VIA PAOLO SARPI, 30
20154 MILANO

+39 02 331 5249
cantineisola.com
Instagram: @cantine_isola

RAVIOLERIA SARPI
VIA PAOLO SARPI, 27
20154 MILANO

laravioleriasarpi.com
Instagram: @laravioleriasarpi

MO SARPI

> Just a short walk away, the historic **Macelleria Sirtori** (Sirtori butchery) offers beef tartare and carpaccio, legendary *mondeghili* (typical Milanese meatballs) with soy sauce, long skewers of spiced beef, and many other specialities to enjoy on the go or seated at the large communal table.

> Another staple of Chinese street food is **Mo Sarpi**, a real gem for those who love to discover lesser-known recipes from Asian street food. Don't miss the Mo, a kind of sandwich stuffed with organic pork which gave the restaurant its name.

> Extend your evening at **PolyGram KTV Karaoke**, a hub for immersing yourself in Asian culture until late at night: private booths, drinks, and songs to sing with friends might just make you the stars of the neighbourhood.

	MACELLERIA SIRTORI VIA PAOLO SARPI, 27 20154 MILANO		MO SARPI VIA PAOLO SARPI, 25 20154 MILANO	
	+39 02 342 482		Instagram: @mosarpi	

MACELLERIA SIRTORI

HUA CHENG

> For an authentic Chinese restaurant experience, head to **Hua Cheng**, a simple and welcoming place with shared tables and genuine dishes. They don't take reservations, but the wait is worth it, especially for the pak choi or the freshly sautéed noodles.

POLYGRAM KTV KARAOKE
VIA PAOLO SARPI, 33
20154 MILANO

polygramktv.com
info@polygramktv.com

HUA CHENG
VIA GIORDANO BRUNO, 13
20154 MILANO

+39 02 345 1613
Instagram: @huacheng_milano

A RELAXING
OASIS OF WELLBEING

Tucked within the 16th-century Spanish walls of Porta Romana, QC Milano is a breathtaking wellness retreat well worth a visit. With around 30 different experiences and treatments, it offers everything from multiple pools and jacuzzis to themed relaxation rooms, multi-sensory experiences (a cinema sauna, a tropical rain hammam, and more), massages, and even a sauna inside a vintage tram.

On sunny days, the outdoor garden is a true delight. It's easy to spend a relaxing half-day or evening here. A decent buffet is available on-site.

 QC MILANO
PIAZZALE MEDAGLIE D'ORO, 2
CORNER VIALE FILIPPETTI
20135 MILANO

+39 02 8974 7205

Instagram: @qcterme

ARIANTEO

ANTEO NELLA CITTÀ

THE MAGIC OF
OUTDOOR CINEMA

Watching a film under the stars is one of Milan's great summertime pleasures. Luckily, **AriAnteo** hosts open-air screenings in stunning locations across the city, from the historic courtyard of Palazzo Reale to the beautiful Chiostro dell'Incoronata and Piazza Elsa Morante, set against the striking skyline of the CityLife district (with skyscrapers designed by Daniel Libeskind and Zaha Hadid).

Another fantastic project, **Anteo nella Città**, brings cinema to unexpected corners of Milan. A van travels through different neighbourhoods, unloading 200 seats, a giant screen, and a projector, with sound transmitted via headphones for an immersive experience.

When the weather cools, Milan is also home to charming independent cinemas like **Cinema Beltrade** and **Il Cinemino**.

ARIANTEO
To find out the locations and times see:
spaziocinema.info

CINEMA BELTRADE
VIA NINO OXILIA, 10
20127 MILANO
cinemabeltrade.net
Instagram: @cinemabeltrade

IL CINEMINO
VIA SENECA, 6
20135 MILANO
ilcinemino.it
Instagram: @ilcinemino

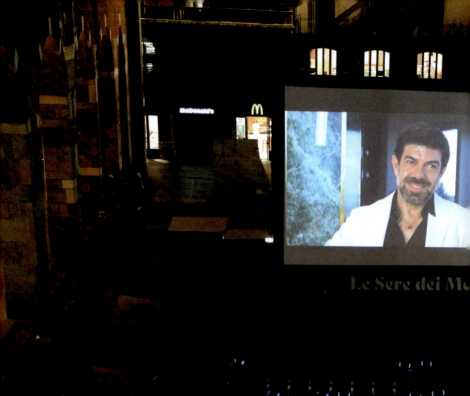

PRE-DINNER DRINKS
AT A GREENGROCER'S

Opened in 1919, after years of wandering, Il Verzeratt found its home in the shade of the charming Basilica of San Nazaro in Brolo. Now run by the fourth generation, this historic kiosk is a beloved Milanese institution, selling fresh fruit and vegetables – but that's not all. In recent years, it has expanded its offerings to include smoothies and fruit salads, served at small outdoor tables.

IL VERZERATT 1919
VIA OSTI, 2
20122 MILANO

+39 02 805 7784

Instagram: @verzeratt

On warm days, you'll also find fresh dishes like caprese and prosciutto with melon, perfect for a light lunch.

On summer evenings, this quiet corner of the city is transformed into an irresistibly charming aperitivo spot just behind the Duomo. From 7pm, the Renaissance façades of Largo Richini come alive, filled with laughter, conversation, and the clinking of glasses.

The highlight? Special cocktails made with freshly squeezed grapefruit juice, expertly prepared at a counter crafted from an old bicycle that once carried coal.

A true slice of Milanese magic.

A HAIRCUT BY CANDLE FLAME
TO STRENGTHEN THE ROOTS

Founded in 1904 on Via Manzoni, Barbieria Colla has moved around Milan over the years, but has always remained a go-to spot for artists and audiences of La Scala. Since 1944, it has been nestled in its historic location on Via Gerolamo Morone, unchanged in appearance, with vintage furnishings and a range of in-house grooming products.

Among its most intriguing techniques for beard, moustache, and hair care is the candle-cutting ritual – an old-school spectacle that draws curious visitors from around the world. After a careful trim with scissors and comb, a candle flame is passed over the freshly cut ends. According to the barbers, the heat seals the keratin, strengthening the hair's structure.

The shop truly comes to life on the day of La Scala's grand opening each year, buzzing like a stage itself, as actors, singers, and fans gather in a lively tribute to its deeply Milanese soul.

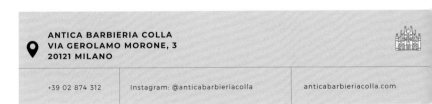

ANTICA BARBIERIA COLLA
VIA GEROLAMO MORONE, 3
20121 MILANO

+39 02 874 312 Instagram: @anticabarbieriacolla anticabarbieriacolla.com

EXCEPTIONAL MODERN ARCHITECTURE
HOUSING ETRUSCAN ART

On Corso Venezia, opposite the Indro Montanelli Gardens, the Luigi Rovati Foundation is a unique gem that houses over 250 Etruscan artworks within an exceptional underground space inspired by the Etruscan tombs of Cerveteri. This cultural treasure is outstanding with its extraordinary underground museum, and was awarded the prestigious Compasso d'Oro ADI 2024 in the 'Exhibition Design' category. This is a rare accolade for a museum whose winding, curved space transforms archaeology into an immersive and poetic experience.

FONDAZIONE LUIGI ROVATI
CORSO VENEZIA, 52
20121 MILANO

fondazioneluigirovati.org
Instagram: @fondazioneluigirovati

Free entry every first Sunday of the month

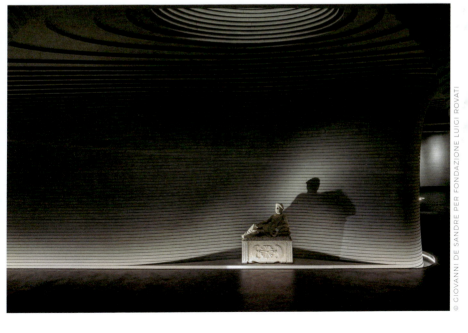

The star of the show is the Etruscan collection, featuring large bucchero vases, gold jewellery, funerary urns, bronzes, and unique pieces displayed in exquisite triangular showcases that narrate the history of one of the world's most refined civilisations.

On the *piano nobile*, 18th-century woodwork and mirrors blend harmoniously with contemporary art.

The palace also features a well-curated bookstore, along with a café-bistro overlooking the garden, and the gourmet restaurant of Michelin-starred chef Andrea Aprea.

THE BEST TRATTORIA IN TOWN?

Founded by long-time friends Pietro Caroli and Diego Rossi, **Trippa Milano** is one of Milan's most beloved trattorias, where creativity meets an informal atmosphere reminiscent of traditional establishments.

Chef Diego's menu changes daily, reflecting seasonality and sustainability while highlighting the iconic dishes that define this eatery. From a contemporary take on *vitello tonnato* – featuring a delicately sweet sauce prepared with a syphon – to crispy fried tripe and mouth-watering butter and parmigiano tagliatelle, every offering showcases a strong identity that pays homage to Italian cuisine. With its warm ambience and excellent wine selection, Trippa is a must-visit for anyone seeking authenticity. Reservations are essential and should be made well in advance.

TRIPPA MILANO
VIA GIORGIO VASARI, 1
20135 MILANO

+393 27 668 7908

trippamilano.it
Instagram: @trippamilano

For those who couldn't get a reservation, part of the Trippa family (Diego Rossi), joined by Josef Khattabi from Kanpai and Frangente restaurants as well as Enricomaria Porta, opened **Osteria alla Concorrenza** in 2021. Located right in the middle of Via Melzo, one of the city's hottest streets for food lovers, the restaurant serves delicious small plates to share alongside fine wines. With room for just 25 people in a snug, welcoming space, you'll be surrounded by bottles (over 1,500 unusual wines!) and authentic 1950s flooring. This is an absolute favourite.

OSTERIA ALLA CONCORRENZA
VIA MELZO, 12
20129 MILANO

+39 02 9167 2012

Instagram:
@osteria_alla_concorrenza

YOU'LL WANT TO EXPLORE AGAIN, EVEN WHEN IT'S TIME TO LEAVE

At **La Balera dell'Ortica**, you'll find a trattoria, a boccia pitch, a dance school, and an occasional vintage market – all wrapped up in a lively celebration where every dish comes with a dance with your tablemates. Here, you don't have to choose; you can enjoy it all, especially a night that breaks the mould.

From summer through to October, the festive atmosphere spills outdoors under the stars, surrounded by twinkling lights and the enticing aroma of grilled food. In winter, you'll cosy up inside next to the boccia courts.

 LA BALERA DELL'ORTICA
VIA GIOVANNI ANTONIO AMADEO, 78
20134 MILANO

+39 02 7012 8680

Instagram: @laballeradelortica

Originally established as a recreation centre for railway workers in the 1960s, it has long been the vibrant heart of Ortica, an authentic neighbourhood often overlooked by tourists. With its checked red-and-white tablecloths and long communal tables, the setting exudes a friendly, relaxed vibe perfect for unwinding with friends or family.

The menu pays tribute to cherished family flavours featuring homemade lasagna, legendary *arrosticini* with potatoes, and the incomparable *spezzatino* from Mamma Rita – each dish tells a story of heartfelt love. After dinner, why not challenge your friends to a game on the restaurant's two boccia courts? Balls are available on-site, ensuring a fun time for all.

At La Balera, every day is a celebration: the seasonal line-up includes vintage markets and live music nights featuring swing and rockabilly. If you want to get into the groove, boogie-woogie and ballroom dance classes will set the perfect tone.

Just a short stroll away, be sure to pop into the **Mazurka Vintage Shop**, the twins' Balera boutique, to complete your evening with the perfect retro outfit.

⚲ DANCE CLASSES IN LA BALERA	⚲ MAZURKA VINTAGE SHOP VIA ORTICA, 3 20134 MILANO
+39 339 582 4825	Instagram: @mazurka_vintageshop

OVER 35,000 BOOKS
IN A MAGICAL PLACE

Books aren't just for reading – they can be experienced, listened to, and touched. In case you'd forgotten this, the Kasa dei Libri will remind you. Neither a library nor a bookstore, it's a haven for creative minds. Spread across the fifth and sixth floors of a modern building near the Bosco Verticale, this warm and unconventional space is the brainchild of Andrea Kerbaker, a writer and collector who has been curating his collection since childhood. Today, it boasts over 35,000 books. Once private family apartments, the rooms have been transformed into an enchanting and welcoming space open to all.

On the fifth floor lies the heart of the collection – rare books, some over 500 years old, like a precious *Aldina* from the year 1500 (one of the first pocket-sized books), along with quirky finds, signed editions, and the mysterious 'phantom books' – works withdrawn from circulation for being too controversial. The seemingly haphazard arrangement invites visitors to get lost among the shelves and wonder: *How did this book end up here?*

KASA DEI LIBRI
LARGO ALDO DE BENEDETTI, 4
20124 MILANO

+39 02 6698 9018

kasadeilibri.it
Instagram: @kasadeilibri

Free

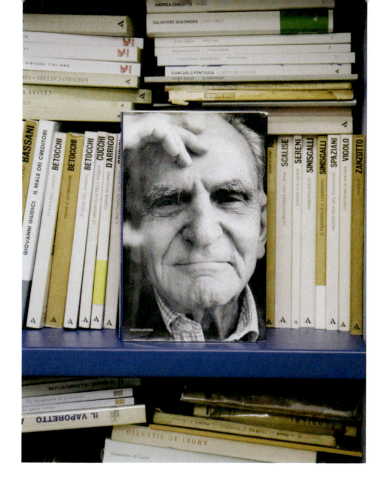

The sixth floor hosts rotating thematic exhibitions, curated from the collection, as well as readings, creative workshops, and discussions for all ages. Entry is completely free, with no reservation required – just ring the doorbell, as if visiting an old friend, and let the books welcome you in. Just like any home worth its name, you'll feel truly welcome. Here, the host isn't a person, but the books themselves – each with more stories to tell than a distant relative. Who knows? Your next favourite book might just be waiting on the top shelf.

MILAN
BY NIGHT

It's an institution, a legendary venue in Milan's nightlife that has taken on a near-mythical status over its forty-year history. Founded on 23 December 1980 at Viale Umbria 120, Plastic earned the title of 'Italy's most European nightclub' in the 1990s, thanks to the visionary music selection of Nicola Guiducci, its historic DJ and sonic mastermind.

A notoriously strict door policy turned the club into a hub of cutting-edge culture, attracting iconic figures from the international scene–though, thankfully, in the past few years, getting in has become a little easier.

PLASTIC CLUB
VIA GARGANO, 15
20139 MILANO

Instagram: @clubplasticmilano

ARCHIVIO PLASTIC

In the 1980s, Andy Warhol was a regular, as was Keith Haring, who wrote in his journal in 1984: 'Plastic is my favourite club in Europe. Nicola [Guiducci] plays music that made me feel like I was in New York.' This fusion of art, fashion, and music remains one of Plastic's defining features, attracting designers, stylists, and up-and-coming artists.

Today, Plastic has relocated to Via Gargano, near Fondazione Prada. The new venue strives to capture the magic of the original club – sometimes tinged with nostalgia – while staying true to its bold identity.

The legend of Killer Plastico (as locals call it) lives on, with a devoted crowd blending old faces and fresh generations. But Plastic is more than just a place to dance – it's a piece of Milan's nightlife history. A cultural laboratory that reinvents itself every weekend.

OTHER MUST-VISIT NIGHTLIFE TEMPLES

> **Apollo Club:** A blend of elegance and effortless cool, perfect for dinner, drinks, and dancing into the night – complete with pole dance bars and a giant disco ball.
Via Giosuè Borsi, 9/2 – 20143 Milano

> **Arca Milano:** With its forward-thinking design, this venue hosts a line-up that often stretches from lunchtime well into the night.
Via Rimini, 38 – 20142 Milano

> **Buka:** No address, no fixed schedule, no set programme – the only certainties at Buka are experimental electronic music, performances, and installations. You just have to be in the right place at the right time.
buka.xyz

> **Detune:** An exciting newcomer rising from the ashes of the historic Atomic Bar. As their Instagram puts it: a hi-fi club with lo-fi memories. Definitely worth a try!
Via Felice Casati, 24 – 20124 Milano

> **Masada**: Somewhere between a club and an art gallery, this venue hosts day-time parties that rewrite Milan's nightlife rules.
Viale Carlo Espinasse, 41 – 20156 Milano

> **Santeria** (Toscana, 31): Bar, restaurant, concert hall, and club – all in one. A guaranteed crowd-pleaser.
Viale Toscana, 31 – 20136 Milano

> **Q Club:** A Berlin-style club vibe – ideal for those seeking an alternative, unconventional night out.
Via Padova, 21 – 20127 Milano

> **Rocket:** A legendary venue once known for showcasing the hottest indie bands. Now based in the Navigli district, its weekends range from futuristic hip-hop to pounding techno.
Alzaia Naviglio Grande, 98 – 20141 Milano

ARCA MILANO
© ARCA MILANO

A UNIQUE, INTIMATE
AND EXTRAORDINARY EXPERIENCE

Among Milan's culinary gems, IYO Omakase stands out as something truly exceptional. Born six years ago as an offshoot of IYO – the first Japanese restaurant in Italy to earn a Michelin star, which it has proudly held since 2015 – this intimate dining spot honours the ancient *omakase* tradition, meaning 'I leave it up to you.'

IYO OMAKASE
PIAZZA ALVAR AALTO / VIALE DELLA LIBERAZIONE, 15
20124 MILANO

+39 02 2506 2828   Instagram: @iyo.omakase   iyo-omakase.com

Just seven seats line the counter, where master sushi chef Masashi Suzuki crafts each bite before serving it directly into the hands of his guests. There's no menu, only trust: every dish is a one-of-a-kind creation, shaped daily by the finest ingredients available.

Even the smallest details delight – like the soy sauce dishes that reveal Mount Fuji when filled, adding to the sense of wonder that defines this remarkable experience.

STREET FOOD,
MILAN STYLE

Milan's food scene is fantastic, of course. But we're not just talking about its restaurants. Here are three essential street food addresses not to be missed.

> Giannasi 1967

Queueing up every Saturday at Giannasi, the king of spit-roasted chicken since 1967 and famous for its green, white and red colours, is part of the ritual of a true Milanese weekend. For generations, Milanese have been coming here for a roast chicken to enjoy at home or on a picnic in one of Milan's parks.

Don't forget to try the Giannuggets too.

GIANNASI 1967
PIAZZA B. BUOZZI, 2
20135 MILANO

+39 320 857 6881

giannasi1967.com
Instagram: @giannasi1967

> **Macelleria Popolare (Darsena)**

Amidst the world's spices and ethnic shops, Darsena hides a wonderful yet unusual butcher.

At Macelleria Popolare, there aren't any butchers, only cooks: the pastrami sandwich, grilled bone marrow and meatballs (polpette della nonna) are among the undisputed bestsellers to be enjoyed standing at the counter or seated facing the Darsena in good weather.

Obviously, you'll find only organic, free-range meats here, cooked in front of you with great care. Don't miss the excellent tiramisu, prepared to order.

MACELLERIA POPOLARE (DARSENA)
PIAZZA VENTIQUATTRO MAGGIO, 4
20123 MILANO

+39 02 3946 8368

> Chiosco Maradona

Unique of its kind, the Maradona Chiosco (kiosk) on Via Tabacchi is the go-to spot in Milan's nightlife for grabbing a bite before finally heading to bed: it doesn't close until everyone is asleep. Here, locals happily enjoy horse meat (but that's not all), sandwiches and massive portions of fries.

Be sure to try the '*Il Magnifico*' sandwich, with horse meat ragù, bacon, onion, scamorza cheese and its knockout secret sauce.

If you're having a late night out in Milan, you'll surely end up at Chiosco Maradona. Don't argue, that's just how it is. It's tradition, and traditions should be respected.

 CHIOSCO MARADONA
VIA ODOARDO TABACCHI, 33
20136 MILANO

| Every day from 9.30pm (until the last customer leaves) | +39 02 3946 8368 | chioscomaradona.it Instagram: @chiosco.maradona |

© GIUSEPPE MACOR

A SECRET TEMPLE
IN A RESTAURANT BASEMENT

Restaurant, temple and Hare Krishna cultural centre, Govinda is a place unknown even to most Milanese. It's more than a restaurant: it's a sanctuary where you can rediscover a fully mindful way of eating.

The real hidden treasure is in the basement: a temple run by the Hare Krishnas, open to anyone wanting to stop for meditation or yoga. You can go before or after lunch, or even while waiting for your meal.

On the ground floor, the traditional Indian food follows the principles of sattvic cuisine, free from meat, fish, eggs, garlic and onions (and alcohol) to purify body and mind. The dishes follow a precise ritual before being served and, it's said, everyone who passes by here will end up eating what they need most, without even realising it.

Aside from being one of Milan's best vegetarian restaurants, Govinda offers a genuine spiritual experience if you truly embrace the concept.

GOVINDA
VIA VALPETROSA, 5
20123 MILANO

+39 02 4941 2043

Instagram: @govinda_milano
@govinda_centro_culturale

VISIT ONE OF THE WORLD'S **MOST BEAUTIFUL LIBRARIES**

Founded in 1770 by Maria Theresa of Austria, the Braidense National Library (or Biblioteca di Brera) is Italy's third national library, after those in Rome and Florence, and one of the most beautiful in the world.

It houses more than 1.5 million volumes including manuscripts, incunabula and precious documents, such as different handwritten versions of Manzoni's *The Betrothed* (*I Promessi Sposi*), the very first editions of Foscolo's texts and even a writing desk that belonged to him.

 BIBLIOTECA NAZIONALE BRAIDENSE
VIA BRERA, 28
20121 MILANO

+39 02 7226 3401

bibliotecabraidense.org
Instagram: @braidense.biblioteca

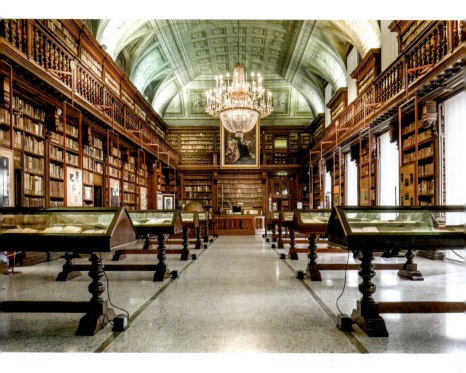

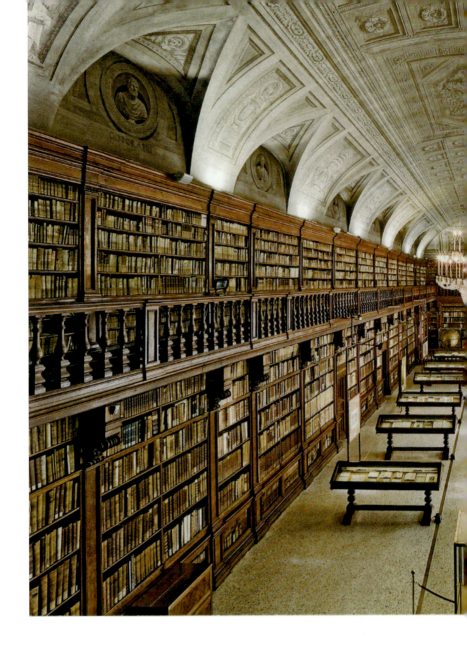

An excellent guided tour takes you through the different rooms: the most beautiful and impressive are the Maria Theresa Hall (also accessible from the Brera Museum when exhibitions are being held there), the Reading Room (accessible

with registration using ID card or passport) and the Catalogue Room.

There is also a Consultation Room (more modern), the small Manzonian Room (for manuscripts) and Umberto Eco's study.

MILAN'S
BEST COCKTAIL BARS

How do you choose an outstanding cocktail bar among Milan's countless drinking spots? Here's a lovely selection of three very different places.

> **1930**

This was the first speakeasy to open in the city 10 years ago; you could only enter if you knew the password and secret address. Now located on Via de Amicis, beneath Mag Pusterla, 1930 continues to be one of Italy's best cocktail bars. According to some, it's even one of the best in the world. In two small 1960s-style rooms, with soft lighting and accompanied by the nostalgic sound of an old jukebox, the highly creative menu will certainly surprise you. To get in: enter the beautiful Pusterla bar and say you're there for '1930'. Grab a drink as you wait, and they might show you the secret entrance. If not, staying at Pusterla is a fine option too!

 1930
VIA EDMONDO DE AMICIS, 22
20123 MILANO

Instagram: @1930cocktailbar

© MARCO MANTA

> **Lom Dopolavoro**

In an old farmhouse dating from 1820, not far from the Monumental Cemetery, Lom Dopolavoro offers a cocktail bar alongside anti-waste vegetarian and vegan cuisine. The atmosphere here provides a tranquil escape from city life.

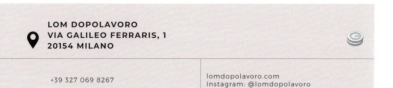

LOM DOPOLAVORO
VIA GALILEO FERRARIS, 1
20154 MILANO

+39 327 069 8267

lomdopolavoro.com
Instagram: @lomdopolavoro

© JULIE COUDER

> **Mœbius**

Named after the famous French illustrator Mœbius, this trendy cocktail bar combines live jazz music, a vinyl shop and two restaurants, one of which has a Michelin star. Don't miss the Pesto Martini, a reinterpretation of the classic martini with Altamura vodka, white balsamic vinegar and homemade pesto. A true must-drink.

MŒBIUS
VIA ALFREDO CAPPELLINI, 25
20124 MILANO

+39 02 3664 3680

Moebiusmilano.it
Instagram: @moebiusmilano

#22

SPEND A DAY LIKE A MILANESE IN THE NAVIGLI DISTRICT

Navigli is one of Milan's liveliest districts: it's young, trendy and alternative. Here are some great addresses for spending a fabulous day while avoiding the crowds of tourists.

Start the day browsing the vintage shops scattered throughout the neighbourhood. There's **Ambroeus Milano** for unearthing timeless pieces (it also has another charming location in the Isola district), **PWC Milano** which mixes pieces from the past with collections from young emerging designers, and finally **Groupies**, a bit further from the centre but perfect for those looking to find vintage treasures from around the world.

At lunchtime, **Brutto Anatroccolo** is a no-frills historic restaurant where time seems to have stood still and the menu is handwritten. The ideal spot to savour budget-friendly Milanese home cooking. Don't miss the mega portion of grilled scamorza and the *arrostino*, when they're available. A rare authentic place.

VINTAGE BOUTIQUES

Instagram:
@ambroeus.milano
@pwcmilano
@groupiesvintage

BRUTTO ANATROCCOLO
VIA EVANGELISTA TORRICELLI, 3
20136 MILANO

+39 02 832 2222

BRUTTO ANATROCCOLO

Since 1982, **Frizzi e Lazzi** has been a bar whose large inner courtyard (hidden from the street) is overlooked by the balustrade buildings of old Milan. A few sandwich options (the '*Cosacco*' is the regulars' favourite), draught beers and big screens for football match evenings await …

For dinner, **Osteria Conchetta** is a neighbourhood institution. The risottos are excellent, particularly the *riserva mantecato* prepared in front of you. Accompanying it with the house's signature 'elephant ear' is almost a tradition. The portions are huge, perfect for sharing with friends.

FRIZZI E LAZZI
VIA EVANGELISTA
TORRICELLI, 5
20136 MILANO

+39 02 837 8228
Instagram: @frizzielazzimilano

OSTERIA CONCHETTA
VIA CONCHETTA, 8
20136 MILANO

+39 02 8372 917
osteriaconchetta.it

After dinner, whether it's 6pm or 11pm, going to **Cox18** means entering a social space, occupied and self-managed since 1976. This is a place that escapes definitions because it simply refuses to be categorised. Creative, artistic, revolutionary, you'll fall in love with this venue because it always has an exciting cultural event to offer, and serves some of the cheapest beer in Milan. On its exterior walls is one of the rare Milanese works by Blu, perhaps the best Italian street artist who, like Banksy, has never revealed his identity.

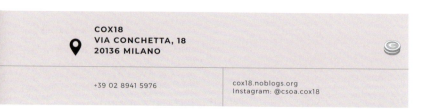

COX18
VIA CONCHETTA, 18
20136 MILANO

+39 02 8941 5976

cox18.noblogs.org
Instagram: @csoa.cox18

I NAVIGLI

A BRILLIANT PIZZERIA
FROZEN IN THE 1970S

Born in the 1970s, Pizzeria Oceania is a unique gem in Milan: vintage '70s decor (in the back room), experimental music playing in the background, pizza cooked in a pan …

Add to this a brilliant red-haired pizzaiolo/owner who will enthusiastically tell you about the artistic installations his father designed when creating the place (of which some traces remain), and you'll understand that it's a bit of the soul of another Milan that you'll find here, in the eastern part of the city centre.

Don't miss the ginger and honey fries or the goulash evenings (you can discover the schedule by bribing the owner!).

An essential stop for anyone seeking an authentic, off-the-beaten-track atmosphere.

  PIZZERIA OCEANIA
   VIA GIOVANNI BRIOSI, 10
   20133 MILANO

+39 349 234 2347

LISTEN TO AN IMPROVISED CONCERT
IN A BOOKSHOP

Hidden in a basement on Via Vettabbia, the Libreria Birdland is much more than a simple bookshop: in a room that's open to everyone, you'll regularly find customers playing the piano while others join in singing. Some may try out a rare score discovered on the shelves, while others will simply give an impromptu little concert.

The idea of opening a bookshop entirely dedicated to jazz was born in New York, home of the legendary jazz club dedicated to Charlie Parker, nicknamed 'Bird' or 'Yardbird', from which the bookshop gets its name.

Today, between the crammed bookshelves, New York-style exposed brick, soft lighting and creaking wooden floors, Birdland has expanded to rock, blues, pop, classical music and opera, with more than 35,000 titles, including hard-to-find scores and out-of-print books.

 LIBRERIA BIRDLAND
VIA VETTABBIA, 9
20122 MILANO

+39 02 5831 0856

birdlandjazz.it
Instagram: @libreriabirdland

UNDERGROUND CULTURE
THAT IS LITERALLY UNDERGROUND

Located in the underpass of the Cairoli M1 stop, LINEA is an underground creative hub, a meeting space, a crossroads of ideas, sounds and people. It's a place defined by its philosophy rather than its appearance.

Between Booth Radio live streams, cultural conferences and art installations, at LINEA people usually arrive by chance or through word of mouth, and end up staying because something unexpected is always happening. It's also an independent shop, ideal for discovering T-shirts, posters, books and vinyl records, and taking home a fragment of Milan that's anything but ordinary.

 LINEA
UNDERPASS OF CAIROLI
METRO STOP - MILANO

linea.media   Instagram: @linea_milano

#26

A RESTAURANT THAT HAS STOOD **THE TEST OF TIME**

There are places that seem to resist everything: trends, social media and the passing of time. Blitz is one of those places.

And there's Antonello, known as Nello, the heart of Blitz. He's never had a telephone or an Instagram account, but everyone knows where to find him. He recites the menu from memory, without lists or written notes. If you listen carefully, it's a piece of theatre. But if you allow yourself to be distracted, you may risk missing a masterpiece. He took all the photos which are hanging on the walls: pictures of famous people from the Italian and international jet set who feel right at home here, enjoying great food and conversation. Not to be missed: the onion soup, the pâté and the snails are all great classics on the menu.

Dinner is served until one in the morning, then people stay at the counter with a glass of myrtle liqueur, while Nello washes the dishes and prepares the place for the next day. Blitz is his home as well as a sanctuary for anyone who appreciates the authenticity of simple things.

BLITZ
VIA CENISIO, 9
20154 MILANO

+39 02 312 388

VISIT AN EXCEPTIONAL MUSEUM
WITHOUT THE CROWDS

Are you fed up with having to elbow hordes of tourists just to catch a glimpse of the masterpieces at the Brera Museum, but you're still keen on seeing some beautiful pieces of art? Welcome to the Bagatti Valsecchi Museum, probably Milan's most fascinating museum.

Opened in 1994 (the heirs lived in the house until 1974), the museum owes its existence to the brothers Fausto and Giuseppe Bagatti Valsecchi who, in the late 19th century, collected Italian masterpieces from the 14th to the 17th century with almost obsessive dedication (paintings, furniture, tapestries, scientific instruments, skulls and globes, etc.), and transformed their home on Via Gesù into a genuine Italian Renaissance palace.

This hidden treasure is well worth a visit, and you'll most likely have the place practically to yourself without the usual tourist throngs. Absolute bliss.

MUSEO BAGATTI VALSECCHI
VIA GESÙ, 5
20121 MILANO

+39 02 7600 6132

museobagattivalsecchi.org
Instagram: @museobagattivalsecchi

CLASSIC
MILANESE CUISINE

Risotto, osso buco, veal Milanese (known locally as *cotoletta*)... If you're looking to discover or rediscover the classics of Milanese cuisine, here are two historic establishments that prepare them to perfection. They'll even make those who've never really liked veal Milanese fall in love with it. Trust us on this one!

> **Trattoria del Nuovo Macello**

Since 1959, Nonna Maddalena's old recipes have been celebrated and reinterpreted in the kitchens of Trattoria del Nuovo Macello, with a contemporary twist. The *risotto alla milanese* is one of the best in the city, so creamy that you'll immediately want to order it again as soon as you finish it. Not to be missed either is the veal Milanese, made with meat that has been aged for forty days, with or without the bone, and available in half portions too. If it's your first visit, the tasting menu is almost as essential as requesting a table in the downstairs dining room. A true delight.

 TRATTORIA DEL NUOVO MACELLO
VIA CESARE LOMBROSO, 20
20127 MILANO

+39 02 5990 2122

trattoriadelnuovomacello.it
Instagram: @trattoriadelnuovomacello

> Trattoria Masuelli San Marco

Passed down from father to son over three generations since 1921, Trattoria Masuelli San Marco offers the best *cotoletta* in the city: thin, crispy and perfectly golden as it should be. This trattoria embodies the near-reverent attention to traditional cooking that continues to thrive throughout Milan. Their *cotoletta* is so delicious it will convert even those who never fancied veal Milanese before.

**TRATTORIA MASUELLI SAN MARCO
VIALE UMBRIA, 80
20135 MILANO**

+39 02 5518 4138

masuellitrattoria.com
Instagram: @trattoriamasuelli

20TH-CENTURY ART
AT YOUR FINGERTIPS

Step through the door of Robertaebasta and you're crossing the threshold of a gallery where every exhibited work can become yours: an avant-garde collection featuring the most celebrated international artists of the 20th century.

Roberta Tagliavini founded her first gallery in Milan in 1967, at a time when the city was very different from today. 'Milan was filthy back then', she recalls frankly. But she was able to see beyond this and helped transform Brera into one of the city's most coveted neighbourhoods.

Her first clients were the fashion greats – those with a knack for staying ahead of the curve. Armani – still a loyal customer today – Cavalli, Versace. 'Versace was actually the very first person to walk in and make a purchase at our Brera shop', Roberta points out. Since those early days, her path has led her to become an international authority, specialising in Art Nouveau and Art Deco, spanning the entire 20th century.

ROBERTAEBASTA
VIA FIORI CHIARI, 2
20121 MILANO

+39 02 861 593

robertaebasta.com
Instagram: @galleria_robertaebasta

Today, with her son Mattia Martinelli, who grew up surrounded by the most iconic artworks of the 20th century, she has expanded her horizons by opening other establishments in Milan and London.

Roberta possesses that rare gift for spotting beauty before it becomes fashionable: 'I've always been fortunate enough to discover certain pieces before others catch on, which means I can buy at better prices. Then, once they become sought-after and prices soar, I simply move on to the next thing', she confides.

Milan embraced Roberta Tagliavini in the 1980s, and Brera became her true home. Even now, you'll find her here every morning, standing with a coffee in her hand. When she's not in the gallery, she's on the television programme Cash or Trash, where her insight into the value and history of objects has found a new audience.

For Roberta, 'being surrounded by beautiful things nourishes the soul'. You'll leave Robertaebasta with a spring in your step and, if your wallet stretches that far, with a one-of-a-kind treasure that will remind you of this feeling every time you look at it in your home.

INTERVIEW

- ROBERTA TAGLIAVINI -
BRERA'S MERCHANT OF ANTIQUITIES AND ART

Where does your passion for art come from?

I started at 16, without a penny to my name. My husband sold coffins, and I designed a line of furniture. What's amusing is that I now often find the furniture we made back then at flea markets. At 21, I opened my first shop in Piazza San Babila with my business partner at the time, Magda, and we called it Roberta and Magda.

Where does the shop name come from?

After ten years of collaboration with Magda, we went our separate ways. At that point, she asked me to remove her name from the shop, which I then called Robertaebasta. I chose this name to make a statement, but I quickly realised it made more of an impression on people. I sold everything off and started selling Art Nouveau pieces, my new passion. I was the first to offer this style in Italy.

Why the Brera district?

In 1980 I left Piazza San Babila because the cost of leases had skyrocketed and the city centre had become dangerous: in those years, there were violent political clashes in the streets. I didn't feel safe on Piazza San Babila. Brera was cheap but very dirty: a rather run-down suburban neighbourhood basically. I was definitely among the first to have contributed to transforming Brera, which eventually became a hot spot for everyone.

When you opened your new gallery, how did Milan and the neighbourhood react?

At first, not everyone liked what I had to offer, except the tailors and fashion designers. Later, newspapers also began asking me for pieces for photo shoots. Then came the films: from *Ocean's Twelve* to *The Great Gatsby* and even *House of Gucci*. Only later did the big industrialists, then private individuals, begin to arrive.

A place in Milan that perfectly embodies the spirit of the city?

Brera, no question about it. In fact, the Brera district resembles me: a bit mad, disorderly, creative, full of life. It's noisy and I like that. It's not a sterile place.

What time of day do you enjoy most in the gallery?

I love the early mornings: I arrive at 8:30, I arrange objects, look at the accounts, prepare an exhibition, make drawings … Morning is my most creative time. Sforza Castle, just a stone's throw from here, is beautiful at 8 o'clock. I always go there with my dog for a quiet walk because it's as if, for a moment, it was just us.

What's the piece you bought that you like best?

There are too many to put in any sort of order! I never fixate on just one thing, it's a constant variation. That's the beauty of this profession: being able to choose and even create trends. I paid 60 million lire (about 30,000 euros) for a Boetti painting, and today one of his paintings is worth a million euros. Nobody teaches you how to anticipate. When I see a new object and it gives me a shiver, I know it's going to work. I love the thrill of buying, but that pleasure ends the moment I pay. Then it's time to work on getting a cheque in and making the sale!

What's your favourite Milanese tradition?

Milan keeps its word. Milan is like me: pragmatic, vibrant, welcoming, hardworking and never tired.

Advice for someone who wants to discover Milan?

You never get tired of observing it. Milan is beautiful everywhere: in its alleyways, in its courtyards, the most beautiful in the world. This city doesn't show off like Rome; in Milan you have to enter it. Open a door and discover a world.

A LITTLE-KNOWN **RENAISSANCE MASTERPIECE**

Built between 1462 and 1468 within the Basilica of Sant'Eustorgio for the Florentine banker Pigello Portinari, an agent of the Medici Bank in Milan, the Portinari Chapel is an overlooked Lombard Renaissance masterpiece that you simply must not miss.

At the heart of the chapel lies the impressive tomb of Saint Peter Martyr, crafted in 1336 by the renowned sculptor Giovanni di Balduccio, and which immediately captures your attention. The cherry on the top? You'll likely find yourself almost alone in this remarkable space.

Particularly noteworthy are the eight female figures perched on various animals, some of which are mythological, symbolising the virtues that the soul must cultivate to achieve spiritual elevation. Also, don't miss the magnificent frescoes adorning the chapel walls, painted by Vincenzo Foppa between 1464 and 1468, as well as the spectacular frescoes on the interior of the dome.

 CAPPELLA PORTINARI
PIAZZA SANT'EUSTORGIO, 3
20122 MILANO

chiostrisanteustorgio.it

ACKNOWLEDGMENTS

To **MILAN**, because if it hadn't allowed itself to be befriended, along with its inhabitants, I would never have been able to discover and rediscover it with you.

To **OTTAVIO FANTIN**, a photographer of great talent, who rediscovered the pleasure of capturing moments with passion thanks to this guide. Thank you for your patience, all the advice you shared with me and the travel adventures we experienced together – now you know the way, it's impossible to get lost.

To **THOMAS JONGLEZ**, thank you for having believed in my ideas, daring as they may sometimes have been, from the get-go, and for allowing me to bring this precious book to life.

To **FEDERICO ESPOSITO** and **MARTA FALCON**, thank you for your wise writing advice and constant sharing of our Milan.

To **MADO DE LA QUINTINIE, EMMANUELLE TOULEMONDE** and all the translators and proofreaders involved, thank you. Without you, this book would not be able to spread its wings and travel the four corners of the world.

And finally, to my parents, **GIANFRANCO** and **GRAZIELLA**, who introduced me to the world and its most remote places before I could even speak, and to my uncle **DARIO**, who always made me travel through the mind. A warm thank you for your courage, and for teaching me to love life.

This book was created by:
Margherita Devalle, author – @margherita_devalle
Ottavio Fantin, photographer
Olivia Fuller, translation
Sigrid Newman, editing
Jana Gough, proofreading
Emmanuelle Willard Toulemonde, layout
Thomas Jonglez and Mado de La Quintinie, publishing

Map: © Sacha Doubroff
Cover: © Ottavio Fantin
Backcover: © Ikeskinen et © CreativePinkBird - AdobeStock

You can write to us at info@editionsjonglez.com
Follow us on Instagram: @editionsjonglez

THANKS

From the same publisher

Photo Books

Abandoned America: The age of Consequences
Abandoned Asylums
Abandoned Australia
Abandoned Belgium
Abandoned Churches: Unclaimed Places of Worship
Abandoned Cinemas of the World
Abandoned France
Abandoned Germany
Abandoned Lebanon
Abandoned Italy
Abandoned Japan
Abandoned Spain
Abandoned USSR
Abandoned World - An AI-generated exploration
After the Final Curtain: The Fall of the American Movie Theater
After the Final Curtain: America's Abandoned Theaters
Baikonur - Vestiges of the Soviet Space Program
Cinemas - A French Heritage
Chernobyl's Atomic Legacy - 25 years after disaster
Clickbait - A visual journey through AI-generated stories
Destination: Wellness - Our 35 best places in the world to make a pause
Forbidden Places - Exploring our Abandoned Heritage
Forbidden France
Forgotten Heritage
Private Islands for Rent
Oblivion
Secret Sacred Sites
Unusual Hotels Europe
Unusual Hotels - World
Unusual Hotels UK & Ireland
Unusual Nights in Paris
Unusual Shopping in Paris
Unusual Wines
Venice deserted

'Soul of' Guides

Soul of Amsterdam - A guide to the 30 best experiences
Soul of Athens - A guide to 30 exceptional experiences
Soul of Barcelona - 30 experiences
Soul of Berlin - A guide to the 30 best experiences
Soul of Brussels - A guide to exceptional experiences
Soul of Detroit - A guide to exceptional experiences
Soul of Kyoto - A guide to exceptional experiences
Soul of Lisbon - A guide to exceptional experiences
Soul of Los Angeles - A guide to 30 exceptional experiences
Soul of Marrakesh - A guide to 30 exceptional experiences
Soul of Marseille - A guide to exceptional experiences
Soul of New York - A guide to 30 exceptional experiences
Soul of Paris - 30 experiences
Soul of Rome - A guide to exceptional experiences
Soul of Tokyo - A guide to exceptional experiences
Soul of Venice - A guide to 30 exceptional experiences
Soul of Vienna - A guide to exceptional experiences

Atlas

Atlas of forbidden places
Atlas of geographical curiosities
Atlas of extreme weather
Atlas of unusual wines

'Secret' Guides

Secret Amsterdam
Secret Bali - An unusual guide
Secret Bangkok
Secret Barcelona
Secret Bars & Restaurants in Paris
Secret Bath - An unusual guide
Secret Belfast
Secret Berlin
Secret Boston - An unusual guide
Secret Brighton - An unusual guide
Secret Brooklyn
Secret Brussels
Secret Budapest
Secret Buenos Aires
Secret Campania
Secret Cape Town
Secret Copenhagen
Secret Corsica
Secret Dolomites
Secret Dublin - An unusual guide
Secret Edinburgh - An unusual guide
Secret Florence
Secret French Riviera
Secret Geneva
Secret Glasgow
Secret Granada
Secret Helsinki
Secret Istanbul
Secret Johannesburg
Secret Lisbon

Secret Liverpool - An unusual guide
Secret London - An unusual guide
Secret London - Unusual Bars & Restaurants
Secret Los Angeles - An unusual guide
Secret Louisiana
Secret Madrid
Secret Mexico City
Secret Milan
Secret Montreal - An unusual guide
Secret Naples
Secret New Orleans - An unusual guide
Secret New York - An unusual guide
Secret New York - Curious Activities
Secret New York - Hidden Bars & Restaurants
Secret Normandy
Secret Paris
Secret Postdam
Secret Prague
Secret Provence
Secret Rio
Secret Rome
Secret Seville
Secret Singapore
Secret Stockholm
Secret Sussex - An unusual guide
Secret Tokyo
Secret Tuscany
Secret Venice
Secret Vienna
Secret Washington DC - An unusual guide

Follow us on Facebook and Instagram

In accordance with regularly upheld French jurisprudence (Toulouse 14-01-1887), the publisher will not be deemed responsible for any involuntary errors or omissions that may subsist in this guide despite our diligence and verifications by the editorial staff.
Any reproduction of the content, or part of the content, of this book by whatever means is forbidden without prior authorisation by the publisher.

© JONGLEZ 2025
Registration of copyright: May 2025 – Edition: 01
ISBN: 978-2-36195-831-2
Printed in Slovakia by Polygraf